T0142621

SEXUAL ASSAULT
A–Z
FROM

A Guide to Terminology and Resources for Survivors and their Allies

Trissa Dodson, *Finding Autonomy,*
Collage on Paper, 2018

ANNIE NOVOTNY

© 2023 Annie Novotny. All rights reserved.

No part of this book may be reproduced, stored in a retrieval system, or transmitted by any means without the written permission of the author.

AuthorHouse™
1663 Liberty Drive
Bloomington, IN 47403
www.authorhouse.com
Phone: 833-262-8899

Because of the dynamic nature of the Internet, any web addresses or links contained in this book may have changed since publication and may no longer be valid. The views expressed in this work are solely those of the author and do not necessarily reflect the views of the publisher, and the publisher hereby disclaims any responsibility for them.

This book is printed on acid-free paper.

ISBN: 979-8-8230-0183-0 (sc)
ISBN: 979-8-8230-0184-7 (e)

Library of Congress Control Number: 2023903302

Print information available on the last page.

Published by AuthorHouse 07/20/2023

authorHOUSE®

This publication is dedicated to the survivors.

ACKNOWLEDGEMENTS

Many mentors, advisors, editors, artists, and friends have lent their insight and creativity to this project. I would like to thank especially the creative direction of Cathy Moon and Eric Von Haynes and Flatland Press. I am deeply grateful for the editing, advice, and encouragement I received from Allie McCormick and Steven Hollander. I am forever grateful for Muffie Delgado Connelly, whose willingness to engage in long hard conversations, life-giving collaborations, and dear friendship have emboldened me to create this book. This book was made possible by the collaboration and support of my cohort(s) within the Art Therapy department at The School of the Art Institute of Chicago and the artists who contributed artwork for this endeavor: Mikey Anderson, Neha Bhat, Annie Chang, Trissa Dodson, Allison Dowd, Toni Eldimere, Beth Enterkin, Jordan Ferranto, Christina Heyworth, Robert Narciso, Cathy Moon, Patrick Morrissey, Rochele Royster, Farah Salem, Teresa "T" Sit, and Danyah Subei- thank you for sharing your creativity to illustrate this often tough text. In addition, I have had the great fortune to have been supported by the mentorship of my supervisors and guides: Beth Enterkin, Jordan Ferranto, Barbara Fish, Patrick Morrissey, Rochele Royster, and the ever- grounding, Suellen Semekoski. I am grateful for my family for their unrelenting support: my original teacher and guide- my mom- Mary Novotny, my father Thomas Novotny who taught me the importance of choosing my battles, my brother Tom who has always had my back, Glenn Edward Jeffries for his support and care, my husband, Robert Jeffries for being always at my side, my "cousin / sister" Rebecca Schedin, and my children Lou Lou and Ayla who inspire me to contribute to the movement toward creating a less violent world for Women. I am grateful to my extended family and chosen family alike- including but not limited to Gabrielle Grotta Hendrickson and Mary DaVanon who are my true allies and supported me fully in my time of need. I would like to thank the advocate who's name I did not catch- who held my hand in the ER while I underwent a rape kit- I will never forget the comfort I received from being held in that moment. I feel so much gratitude toward the women who have always been my allies: Colleen O'Sullivan and Nikol Laporta- thank you for (literally) standing up for me, my coven in no particular order: Muffie Delgado Connelly, Colleen O'Sullivan, Rose Rita Walsh, Gina Pannorfi, Chiara No, Ellen Gladish, Kate Mallor, Keelin Mayer, Susannah Donne, Maureen Sorell, and Julie DeLeon- thank you for engaging in the magic with me. This book is directly inspired by the work and efforts of the team of counselors and advocates at Resilience Chicago, fighting the good fight on the frontlines of the Rape Crisis Movement. Lastly- but perhaps most importantly- I am indebted to the countless survivors who have entrusted me with their stories over the past several years. I feel privileged to have had the opportunity to be present for the pain and the healing that you have allowed me to witness. Thank you for letting me walk beside you on your path of survivorship- this book is for you.

WARNING

Please be advised that the subject of this publication is sexual violence. The following pages have detailed and explicit information regarding potentially upsetting material pertaining to sexual assault.

INTRODUCTION

In the aftermath of a sexual assault, it is normal for survivors and those that support them to find it hard to define their experience or put their thoughts and feelings into words. Survivors may come into contact with many different systems that have attempted to create language around the experience of sexual assault. Navigating the responses of the health care system, the legal system, the justice system, as well as family and community systems can be overwhelming and often re-traumatizing for both survivors and their allies. Each system has adopted different language to address sexual violence, depending on the aim of that system. The way in which survivors and their communities define their experiences of sexual violence may differ from the ways in which these systems define sexual violence. Although this publication is not exhaustive, it was the intention of its' creator to gather together a brief but comprehensive guide of common terminology, statistics, and resources relating to the current rape-crisis movement and to shine a light on the potentially confusing landscape of interventions that provide services to survivors. This book is intended to provide information for empowerment and de-stigmatization, to help survivors and their allies make sense of their experience of sexual assault, and to demonstrate to survivors that they are not alone.

Beth Enterkin, *Luminaries*, cut paper, 2017

Annie Novotny, *I Used to Be Fearless,* **Embroidery floss and found fabric, 2019**

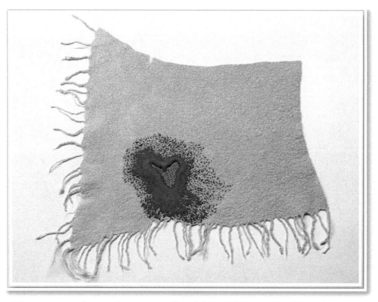

Annie Novotny, *Blown Apart*, **Embroidery floss and found fabric, 2017**

A is for:

Ally is defined as:

to unite or form a connection or relation between: ASSOCIATE
: to form or enter into an alliance [1]

There are many ways to be an ally to; and support a victim of sexual assault:

- o **Allies Never Engage in Victim Blaming:** Sexual assault is a criminal act. Sexual assault is never the victim's fault, but the fault of the perpetrator. See also, "B" for **Believe Survivors**, and "V" for **Victim Blaming**.
- o **Allies Listen with Respect:** It is up to the victim to decide how they want to proceed, following an assault. It is the victim's decision whether or not they want to report an assault. A true ally respects the victim's decision either way, without judgment.[2]
- o **Allies Take Action:** Allies may offer concrete support for victims by helping them connect to support, by making phone calls for them, or by driving them to the hospital, police station and/ or rape crisis center. Allies can also offer to stay with the victim during the medical examination and interviews.[3]
- o **Allies Respond with Empathy:** Most importantly, allies respond with **Empathy** (see 'E') to the person they are supporting.[4]Allies may offer up key phrases, such as "I believe you", "it's not your fault", and "I'm here for you".

- • **The Anti-Rape Movement** is deeply intertwined with the history of slavery in the United States, and the struggle of African American women against racism and sexism. Prior to Emancipation, it was common and acceptable for white slave owners to rape enslaved women. During the period of Reconstruction and the Jim Crow era, sexual violence, physical violence, and murder were used as tactic to terrorize and keep the Black population from gaining political or civil rights. [5] A group of Black women who were raped by a white mob gang during the Memphis Riot of 1886, became the very first women to testify the details of their assaults before congress. Throughout the first half of the twentieth century, women continued to resist through grassroots efforts, but the next wave of anti-rape activities began in the late 1960's and early 1970's on the heels of the Civil Rights and women's liberation movements. 1972 saw the earliest rape crisis centers, established in major cities. At this time, the second wave of feminism brought more white women into the movement. [6] Although **Women of Color** (see 'W') were still at the core of this movement, "their visibility and efforts had been made largely invisible in the absence of critical attention to racism and **Intersectional** (see 'I') analysis in the movement."[7] The anti-rape movement in the U.S. in its' current form is due much in part to the courage and strength of Black women leading the way. Those who currently work within the movement are tasked to pro-actively center the experiences of **Women of Color** and the voices of other marginalized survivors. See also "I" for **Intersectional Feminism,** "M" for **The "Me Too" Movement**, "Q" for **Queer Survivorship**, "X" for **Xenephobia and Sexual Assault**, and 'W' for **Women of Color**.

- **Art Therapy** is a "therapeutic process facilitated by an art therapist, a master's level trained practitioner, that uses art mediums and practices to explore feelings, reconcile emotional conflicts, foster self-awareness, manage behavior, reduce anxiety, and increase self-esteem."[8] When working with survivors of sexual assault, art-based interventions may be used to facilitate the processing and integration of traumatic memories.[9] Art making and the resulting product can act as a container for overwhelming emotions. Art making may be an ideal therapy for trauma survivors because art allows for *Non-Verbal* (see 'N') expression. "The art therapy process engages multiple senses and provides a unique vehicle for expression where words and language can fall short."[10] For more, see "D" for *Dance Movement Therapy*, and "N" for *Non-Verbal Therapeutic Approaches*.

B is for:

- **"Believe Survivors" is a rallying cry.** There are many reasons why a survivor of sexual assault may be reluctant to tell their story. Among these reasons may be the fear of being blamed for the assault or not being believed by anyone. Survivors of sexual assault often have to contend with a pervasive and dominant *Rape Culture* (see 'R') that both promotes and tolerates *Victim Blaming* (see 'V'). Survivors may also be less likely to come forward if there is a significant power difference between the perpetrator and themselves, such as in the case of prominent political figures or religious leaders. One of the most powerful ways *Allies* (see 'A'), can support survivors of sexual assault is to say, "I believe you." In fact, the simple statement, *#BELIEVESURVIVORS*[11] has become a viral rallying cry on social media platforms as the anti-rape movement gains momentum, in the wake of the *#Metoo Movement* (see 'M').[12]

- **Breathing** is a regenerative and restorative process. Focusing on breathing facilitates relaxation and can reset the nervous system. The autonomic nervous system can get stuck in a chronic sympathetic response loop that is commonly known as *Fight-or-Flight* (see 'F') response mode, characterized by short shallow breathes, or periods of holding one's breath.[13] Mindful deep breathing can be very *Grounding* (see 'G') and soothing, allowing one to feel present in their body (see 'E' for *Embodied*), while activating the parasympathetic nervous system. The parasympathetic nervous system (PSNS) promotes self-preservation functions like digestion and wound healing. Once a perceived threat has passed, the PSNS turns down the arousal system, which returns breathing to normal, slows down the heart rate, and relaxes muscle tension. [14] See also "F" for *Fight Flight or Freeze*, and "Y" for *Yoga*.

C is for:

Consent is *to give assent or approval: AGREE* [15]

Before engaging in sexual activities with someone, one needs to gain consent from the other person(s) involved. Without consent, sexual activity (including but not limited to oral sex, genital touching, and vaginal or anal penetration) is sexual assault or rape. Consent is:

o **Freely given-** a choice made without pressure, manipulation, or under the influence of drugs or alcohol.

o **Reversible-** anyone can change their mind about what they feel like doing, at anytime.

o **Informed-** consent can only be given if one has the full story (sexual history of the partner, aware of sexually transmitted infections, understood methods of birth control, etc.)

o **Enthusiastic-** consent is only what one WANTS to do, not what one is expected to do.

o **Specific-** saying yes to one sexual act does not mean yes to all sexual acts.[16]

- **Community and Connection** is essential in the wake of a sexual assault. A survivor of sexual violence may feel anxious, unsafe, and ashamed, which can lead to isolation and depression. Survivors are more likely to process and integrate the trauma of their assault, and heal in relationship to families, friends, community, and *Allies* (see 'A') who provide physical and emotional support, free from judgment and shame.[17] Sexual assault does not occur in a vacuum, and thus entire communities are impacted as the result of sexual violence. Stronger together, communities can join forces to collectively support survivors and confront sexual violence through action. Connecting to a supportive community can help to facilitate the process of *Healing* (see 'H') for survivors after a sexual assault.

Cathy Moon, *I Remember Every Single One of You,* **Acrylic paint and fabric on paper, 1994**

7

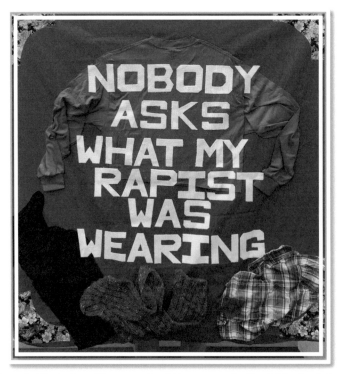

Danyah Subei and Christina Heyworth, *Monument Quilt, Nobody Asks*, Fabric, 2017

Cathy Moon, *Just Walking*, Fabric, 2017

D is for:

- **Dance/movement therapy** (DMT) is defined by the American Dance Therapy Association (ADTA), as the "psychotherapeutic use of movement to promote emotional, social, cognitive, and physical integration of the individual, for the purpose of improving health and well-being."[18] In his book, *The Body Keeps the Score*, Bessel van der Kolk writes that, "being able to perceive visceral sensations is the very foundation of emotional awareness."[19] Dance movement therapy falls under the creative arts therapies umbrella, and like *Art Therapy* (see 'A'), DMT can be an excellent *Non-Verbal* (see 'N'), treatment for people who have experienced sexual trauma. See also "E" for *Embodied*.

- **Date Rape,** also referred to as acquaintance rape, is a sexual assault crime committed by someone who is familiar to or knows the victim. Acquaintance rape includes any forced, manipulated or non-consensual sexual contact. The rapist may be a date, neighbor, boss, co-worker, delivery person, spouse, relative or anyone known to the victim.

  o 77% of rape victims were known to their attackers
  o 90% of acquaintance rape victims do not report their assault to police [20]

- **Disabilities and Sexual Assault:** According to the Department of Justice, a variety of limitations are included under the term "disability". "Due to the fact that people with different disabilities may face different challenges and have very different needs, some disabilities may put people at higher risk for crimes like sexual assault or abuse."[21] *Consent* (see 'C'), is crucial when any person engages in sexual activity, but it plays an even bigger, and potentially more complicated role when someone has a disability. Perpetrators may take advantage of the fact that some disabilities may make it difficult to communicate consent to participate in sexual activity. In addition, someone who has a developmental or intellectual disability may not have the ability to consent to sexual activity, as defined by the state laws.[22] For a number of reasons, "sexual abuse and assault of people with disabilities often goes *Unreported* (see 'U')."[23] According to the National Crime Victimization Survey, there are a variety of reasons a person with disabilities may not report a sexual assault:

  - *Someone who relies on the person abusing them may be reluctant to report the abuse.*
  - *An abuser may block access to the tools a person with a disability uses to communicate, such as a computer or phone.*
  - *People with disabilities may be less likely to be taken seriously when they make a report of sexual assault or abuse. They may also face challenges in accessing services to make a report in the first place.*
  - *Many people with disabilities may not understand or lack information about healthy sexuality and the types of touching that are appropriate or inappropriate. This can be especially challenging if a person's disability requires other people to touch them to provide care.*[24]

- **Dissociation** is defined as a "process of losing a sense of presence resulting in experiencing a disconnection and a lack of continuity between thoughts, memories, surroundings, and actions."[25] Experiencing dissociation during a sexual assault, and / or as a symptom of **PTSD** (see 'P') after the assault has occurred is a normal response to such a traumatic event. Linked to the **"Freeze"** response (see 'F'), dissociation can be experienced as anything from a foggy dream-like state to a feeling of one's mind "going blank", to a "loss of personal identity that can severely impact interpersonal relationships and daily functioning."[26] Dissociation is a defense mechanism that acts as a buffer to protect the person experiencing the trauma from feeling the full force of the intense experience. According to Kolk, "The overwhelming experience [of trauma] is split off and fragmented, so that emotions, sounds, images, thoughts, and physical sensations related to the trauma take on a life of their own." Some people report the experience of dissociation as having an out-of-body experience, witnessing the assault from a third-party point of view. Dissociation can be treated through body-based therapies such as *Dance Movement Therapy* (see 'D') that encourage *Embodiment* (see 'E'), and various *Grounding* (see 'G') techniques, as well as *Yoga* (see 'Y').

- **Domestic Violence,** also referred to as intimate partner violence, is *the willful intimidation, physical assault, battery, sexual assault, and/or other abusive behavior as part of a systematic pattern of power and control perpetrated by one intimate partner against another. Domestic Violence may include physical violence, sexual violence, psychological violence, and emotional abuse. The frequency and severity of domestic violence can vary dramatically; however, the one constant characteristic of domestic violence is one partner's consistent efforts to maintain power and control over the other.*[27] Domestic Violence may include rape or various forms of sexual assault as a means of gaining power over and dominating victims. **For anonymous, confidential help available 24/7, call the National Domestic Violence Hotline at 1-800-799-7233 (SAFE) or 1-800-787-3224 (TTY).**

- **Drug Facilitated Sexual Assault** is the use of drugs by rapists, in order to make their victims defenseless. Drugs used for the purpose of sexual assault may cause the victim to lose mobility and even consciousness. When the victim wakes up, they may not have any memory of being assaulted. This loss of memory can cause a victim to be confused and second-guess what happened to them. The effects of being drugged may be similar to "blacking out" from too many drinks or feel like a bad hangover the next day. If a person thinks they may have been drugged and assaulted, they should seek medical attention and a physical exam. "Date rape" drugs may be used on any gender. "Alcohol is the most commonly used date rape drug. Drugs used to facilitate sexual assault are often colorless, odorless and tasteless, and can be slipped into drinks without detection 50% of acquaintance rapes, involve alcohol consumption by the offender, victim or both."[28] Some common drugs used to spike alcoholic drinks are:

  - **Rohypnol** is the trade name for flunitrazepam.
  - **Clonazepam** (marketed as Klonopin in the U.S. and Rivotril in Mexico)
  - **Alprazolam** (marketed as Xanax).
  - **GHB**, which is short for gamma hydroxybutyric acid
  - **Ketamine**[29]

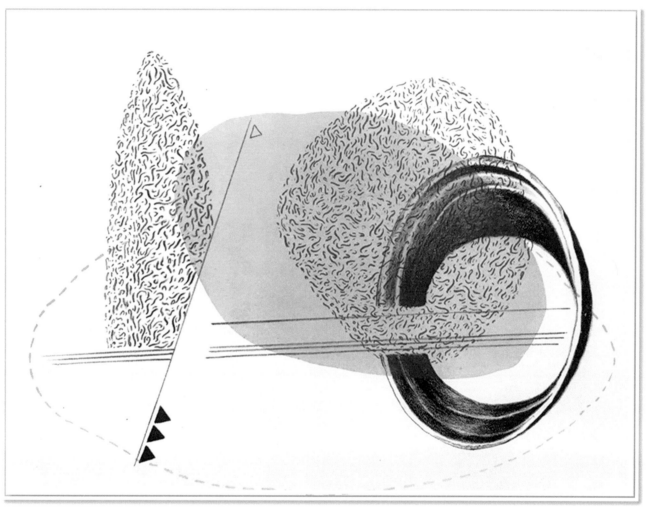

Alison Dowd, *Healing***, Lithograph, 2018**

T. Sit, *My Heart is Gentle and Tender*, Ink on paper, 2021

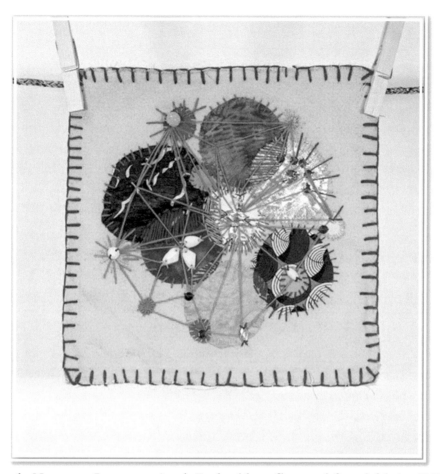

Annie Novotny, *Intergenerational*, Embroidery floss and found fabric, 2019

Annie Novotny, *The Leading Cause of Rape,* Found fabric and thread, 2018

E is for:

- **Embodied** is defined as *"to cause to become a body or part of a body : INCORPORATE"*[30] In his book, *The Body Keeps the Score*, Kolk states that people traumatized by sexual assault often report "feeling unsafe inside their bodies."[31] Survivors of sexual assault often experience various physical symptoms related to the trauma they experienced. Sometimes the symptoms manifest in the form of chronic pain, or numbness and an inability to feel sensations in certain parts of the body. Sexual assault survivors can be overwhelmed by the intrusion of physical symptoms that make up **Rape Trauma Syndrome** (see 'R'). According to Kolk, a person's ability to sense their physical body is directly related to an internal awareness that facilitates agency and a feeling of control over one's own life. It is recommended that survivors of sexual assault connect to body-based therapies, such as working with a **Dance Movement Therapist** (see 'D'), a somatic experiencing specialist, or take up a physical practice such as **Yoga** (see 'Y') in order find ways to safely re-inhabit their body after the trauma of sexual assault, and connect to their internal bodily sensations.

- **Empathy** is: *the action of understanding, being aware of, being sensitive to, and vicariously experiencing the feelings, thoughts, and experience of another of either the past or present without having the feelings, thoughts, and experience fully communicated in an objectively explicit manner.*[32] Cultivating the ability to empathize with another is one of the first steps an **Ally** (see 'A') can take, in order to show up for survivors of sexual assault. Brené Brown, detailed the four main attributes of empathy as the ability "to see the world as others see it, to be nonjudgmental, to understand another person's feelings, and to communicate an understanding of that person's feelings."[33]

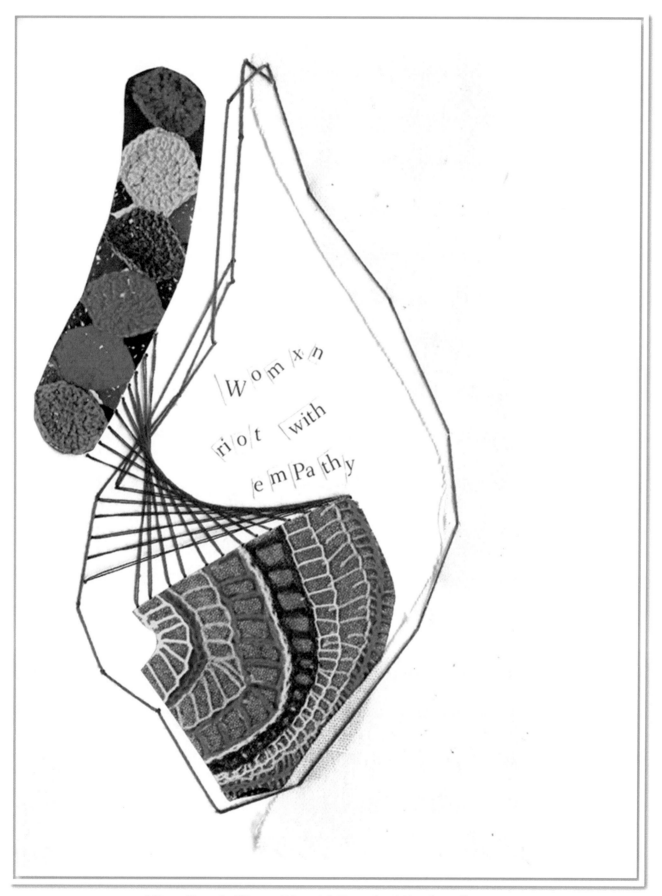

Alison Dowd, *Womxn Riot with Empathy,* **Mixed media, 2017**

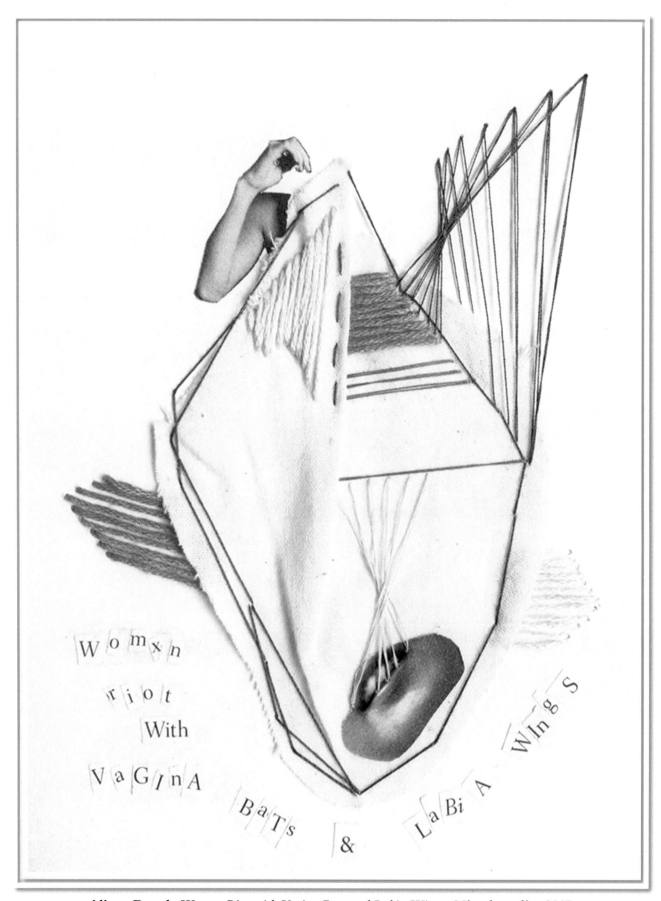

Alison Dowd, *Womxn Riot with Vagina Bats and Labia Wings,* **Mixed media, 2017**

F is for:

- **The Fight, Flight, or Freeze Response** is the term used to describe the survival strategies of a mammal. In order to survive what is perceived as a potentially life-threatening experience, the brain activates the autonomic nervous system response, and hormonal exchanges between the brain and the adrenal glands; mobilize. This activation of neurological and physiological action is referred to as the fight-or-flight response- and is made possible by the sympathetic nervous system (SNS). The SNS moves blood to the muscles for quick action, causes the adrenal glands to squirt out adrenaline, which speeds up the heart rate and increases blood pressure, preparing the body to fight or run.[34] The freeze function acts to preserve life in the face of a threat that cannot be fought off, or escaped from, such as in the case of being physically overpowered or held down.[35] In order to survive the life-threatening event, or potentially feel less pain while being injured, the, "freeze state of an animal or person usually involves some degree of numbness to pain." [36] Although the freeze response is an automatic response, many survivors of sexual assault feel guilt and shame for their body's immobility response. Some survivors feel like they should have or could have done more to fight back or flee the situation, but the autonomic nervous system does not discriminate or assign a hierarchy to these responses. The autonomic nervous system is involuntary- and life preserving- and cannot be controlled cognitively in moments of life or death. See also "D" for ***Dissociation***.

- **Fawn** is a term that was first used by Pete Walker, a C-PTSD survivor and a licensed marriage and family therapist who specializes in working with adults who were traumatized in childhood. "Fawning" has been recognized as an extreme version of "people-pleasing" and a trauma response. According to Walker,

> *Fawn types seek safety by merging with the wishes, needs and demands of others. They act*
> *as if they unconsciously believe that the price of admission to any relationship is the forfeiture*
> *of all their needs, rights, preferences and boundaries.*[37]

When a survivor feels triggered or fearful, they may respond by fawning to appease the perpetrator, and as a means of survival. Fawning may also become a default response for survivors within other interpersonal relationships making them more vulnerable to emotional abuse and exploitation. According to Walker, in circumstances of abuse (for example childhood abuse or intimate partner violence), abusers may suppress a survivor's fight or flight responses by threatening punishment, leading to the survivor's reliance on the fawn or freeze response.[38] See also 'D' for ***Dissociation*** and ***Domestic Violence***.

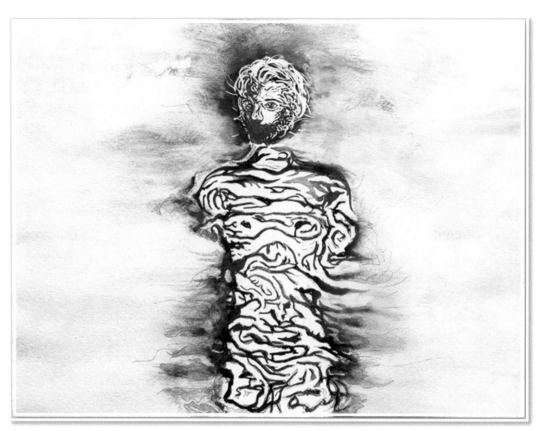

Patrick Morrissey, *Study for Freeze*, **2018, Gouache on paper, 2018**

Neha Bhat, *Neurobiology of Trauma*, **Mixed media on handmade paper, 2018**

G is for:

The term "grounding" refers to any technique that helps keep someone in the present moment when experiencing symptoms such as anxiety, **Dissociation** (see 'D'), or intrusive flashbacks of the traumatic event they experienced in the past. Grounding techniques help reorient a person to the here-and-now of their present reality. They may help someone to regain their mental focus and regulate intense emotions that may arise. Sometimes when a survivor is **Triggered** (see 'T') or begins to experience a flashback of their assault, a grounding technique may help to root them in the present moment and help to activate their parasympathetic response system. See also "E" for **Embodied**.[39]

Some Examples of Grounding Techniques:

- Seated on a chair, firmly plant feet on the floor, eyes may be open or closed. If eyes are open, one may focus the gaze on a single object or focal point. **Breathe** (see 'B') in slowly through the nostrils for the count of three, then exhale out slowly through the nostrils, counting to 5. One may bring one's focus to the body. Siting up tall so the spine is long. Notice the feeling of having contact between the physical body and the chair's surface. One may place their hands on their knees and imagine their legs to be tree trunks. One may imagine roots are growing from one's feet, deep into the earth below the feet. Continue to inhale softly, and exhale fully until one is feeling calm and present.
- A good practice may be keeping a "grounding object" like a smooth stone, or stress ball in one's bag or pocket. When symptoms of anxiety begin, one may find the object and squeeze it- perhaps one may repeat a mantra of "I am safe, I am in the present" in one's head or out loud. One may connect to their breath, by squeezing the object for the count of three while inhaling, and releasing the object for the count of 5, while exhaling.
- One may carry a small bottle of essential oil such as lavender, peppermint, or orange oil, to inhale if they begin to feel anxious or dis-regulated. The scent may help them feel calm, facilitate deep breathing, and orient them to the present moment.[40]
- One may identify 5 things they can see, 4 things they can feel, 3 things they can hear, 2 things they can smell, and 1 thing they can taste. This exercise helps to connect to mindfulness, cognitively distract the mind, and also orient one to the present. Connecting to the breath, and trying to exhale deeply, actives the parasympathetic nervous system.

H is for:

Sexual Harassment is defined as any verbal or physical interaction that is sexual in nature and unwanted. The permissive attitudes toward sexual harassment allows sexism and the objectification of women to continue within the **rape culture** (see 'R') that permeates the society we live within. [41] See also "Z" for **Zero Tolerance**.

Some examples of sexual harassment are:

- o Verbal abuse- jokes or conversations about sex

- o Physical contact that is unwanted including physical assault
- o A sexual suggestion or explicit language about sex that is unwanted
- o Pressure for sex and/ or demanding sexual favors
- o Showing sexually explicit or degrading materials or media
- o A pattern of sexually discriminatory remarks. Harassment can happen at work, at school, or on the street in public spaces. Any unwanted verbal or physical interaction is sexual harassment.

- A **Hotline** is a phone number you can any time to speak with a person who is there to listen and provide support. The National Sexual Assault Hotline number is **1-800-656-4673** which is available 24 hours a day and is free and confidential. Another resource is the Rape and Incest National Network at www.rainn.org, which has detailed information and resources for survivors and their allies.

- **Healing** is possible after a sexual assault. There is no "right" way to react to sexual trauma. There is no set amount of time one is supposed to take in order to "heal" from the trauma of being assaulted. There is no set pathway that leads towards mending and recovery. Every person has their own unique reaction to sexual assault trauma, and everyone has different ways of coping. Wherever a person is on the road to healing, locating a network of supportive people that can offer compassionate attention and **_Empathy_** (see 'E'), is a great place to start. There are Rape Crisis Centers and independent organizations that offer counseling and advocacy, support groups, and resources for survivors and their allies. Survivors and their allies can visit www.rainn.org to find more information and support. [42]

Annie Chang, *Don't Look*, Acrylic, embroidery floss, glitter, plastic food wrap, and found vintage nightie, 2018

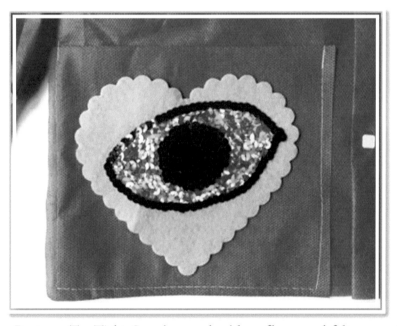

Annie Chang, *Your Pants are Too Tight,* Sequins, embroidery floos, and felt on medical jacket, 2018

I is for:

- **It's Not Your Fault.** Rape is never the victim's fault. It doesn't matter where the victim was at the time of their assault, what they were wearing, or what they were doing. Rape is always the fault of the perpetrator. No matter what the situation is, it is never okay for someone to force a person to engage in sexual acts, or to perform sexual acts on a person who is unable to consent. See "C" for *Consent* and 'V' for *Victim Blaming*.

- **Incest** is sexual relations between family members.

    Relatives may include any family member such as parents, stepparents, siblings, uncles, grandparents and other blood relations as defined by law. Incest constitutes abuse when the child is unable to give informed consent to sexual activity due to the authority of the relative, the child's dependency and lack of power, and/or the difference in ages between the child and the relative. The majority of juvenile victims know the perpetrator, and approximately 34 percent of perpetrators [43] in cases of child sexual abuse are family members.[44]

Studies have shown that the effects of child sexual abuse can be long lasting and affect the victim's mental health later in life.[45] In addition, victims of sexual assault are more likely than non-victims to experience the following mental health challenges:

- About 4 times more likely to develop symptoms of drug abuse
- About 4 times more likely to experience *PTSD* (see 'P') as adults
- About 3 times more likely to experience a major depressive episode as adults"[46]

Survivors of incest anonymous: https://siawso.wildapricot.org/contact.[47]

- **Incarceration and Sexual Assault:** Sexual violence affects thousands of prisoners across the country. An estimated 80,600 inmates each year experience sexual violence while in prison or jail.[48] In addition to interpersonal violence between inmates. According to the Department of Justice, 60% of all sexual violence against female inmates is perpetrated by jail or prison staff. Sexual contact between an inmate and staff member is illegal and can never be consensual. [49] The Prison Rape Elimination Act (PREA) was passed by Congress in 2003. The purpose of the act was to "provide for the analysis of the incidence and effects of prison rape in Federal, State, and local institutions and to provide information, resources, recommendations and funding to protect individuals from prison rape." [50] Due to the extreme power differential between inmate and prison staff, sexual assault in prison often goes unreported. The rape of inmates by other inmates is often overlooked and underreported for fear of retaliation by the perpetrator. See "U" for *Under-Reported* and "I" for *Intersectional Feminism*.

- **Intersectional Feminism** is an analytic framework which attempts to identify how overlapping systems of power impact those who are most marginalized in society.

    *Intersectionality considers that various layers of social identity, such as class, race, sexual orientation, age, disability (see 'D' for **Disabilities and Sexual Assault**), and gender, do* *not exist separately from each other but are interwoven together. While the theory began as an exploration of the oppression of **Women of Color** (see 'W') within society, today the analysis is potentially applied to all social categories (including social identities usually seen as dominant when considered independently).*[51]

When applied to sexual assault, intersectional theory must be used to consider the complex identities of victims. **Women of Color**, such as Black, Latina, and Indigenous women, immigrants, and people who identify within the LGBTQ community, (see 'Q' for **Queer Survivorship)**, who experience sexual violence are less likely to receive services and resources in the after math of the assault. Members of marginalized social groups are at greater risk for experiencing traumatic events, and often experience greater difficulty recovering from such events due to systemic injustice, lack of access to recovery resources, and ineffective services that do not address their unique experiences of trauma.[52] Furthermore, when members of marginalized groups experience sexual violence, it may be considered a hate crime. See "X" for **Xenophobia**. The FBI defines a hate crime as a "committed criminal offense which is motivated, in whole or in part, by the offender's bias(es) against a race, religion, disability, sexual orientation, ethnicity, gender, or gender identity."[53]

J is for:

- **Justice (???)** is: *the administration of law*[54]
  There are many factors to consider when deciding whether to report a sexual assault and engage the criminal justice system. The Vast Majority of Perpetrators Will Not Go to Prison.[55] Out of every 1000 Rapes reported, 994 perpetrators will not be punished for their crime. For these reasons, and various others, the majority of sexual assaults are not reported to the police, (see 'U' for **Under-Reported)**. When a crime is committed, there is a small window of time that a state has to charge the perpetrator. The laws that determine this time frame are called criminal statutes of limitations, and they vary from state to state. When a sexual assault is reported, the "burden of proof" is on the State's Attorney. This means that a perpetrator of sexual assault is innocent until proven guilty by the state. When reporting the crime of sexual assault, the survivor of the assault does not get to press charges. It is the state that would be pursuing the criminal court case. Sexual assault survivors are considered to be *witness / victims* to the crime of sexual assault. Due to the nature of sexual assault, the most substantial proof is usually DNA collected during what is often referred to as *"Rape Kit"* (see 'R'). Even if DNA evidence is collected, the time it takes to process a kit, can take months to years. According to the FBI, "if law enforcement or the prosecution team, feel that they are not able to prove guilt, they may decide not to press charges. Out of every 1000 instances of rape, only 13 cases get referred to a prosecutor, and only 7 cases will lead to a felony conviction."[56] Criminal court proceedings may last several months to years, with no guarantee of a conviction. In addition, if a perpetrator of sexual assault is convicted, there is a very low chance that they will receive any significant access to therapeutic reform while incarcerated. See also "P" for **Perpetrators**.

Farah Salem Alhaidar, *Al–Basirah (plants and palm) from Responding to Violence (plant series)***, Cyanotype photography and embroidery, 2018**

K is for:

- **Kids** are extremely vulnerable to sexual abuse. Child Sexual Abuse is "the sexual exploitation or victimization of a child by an adult, adolescent, or older child."[57] Due to the age difference between an older person and a child, as well as the difference in knowledge and understanding, it is impossible for a child to give informed consent to sexual activity. The term *sexual abuse* includes a wide range of behaviors, including "vaginal, anal, or oral penetration, fondling, exhibitionism, prostitution, and photographing a child for pornography."[58] The sexual abuse of a child does not have to involve force, children are often coerced or bribed to engage in sexual acts.

  According to child protective services agencies, from 2009-2013, 63,000 children a year were victims of sexual abuse.[59] "More than half (54 percent) of female victims and nearly three quarters (71 percent) of male victims were first raped before their 18th birthdays."[60] According to the Department of Health and Human Services:

  - 61% of rape victims were sexually assaulted before the age of 18.
  - One in three girls and one in six boys are sexually abused before the age of 18.
  - Over a third of all sexual assaults involved a victim who was under the age of 12.
  - Of the 22.3 million adolescents in the United States today, 1.8 million have been victims of serious sexual assault.[61] See also, 'I' for **Incest**.

L is for:

- A **Legal Advocate** is someone who knows and understands the law, and who represents and supports the interests of a survivor within the legal system. Navigating the criminal justice system can be overwhelming and potentially re-traumatizing (see 'J' for **Justice???**). Legal advocates may be called upon so that victims do not have to be alone during what can often be a lengthy and difficult process. Legal advocates champion for the rights of survivors, acting as a liaison with law enforcement and prosecutors, throughout court proceedings. Advocates may be connected to through organizations recommended by the State's Attorney, Rape Crisis Centers, and other independent organizations.

M is for:

- **Male Survivorship** is a term used to refer to male-identifying persons who have experienced sexual assault. Sexual assault can happen to anyone of any age, sexual orientation, or gender identity. Due to social attitudes and stereotypes surrounding masculinity, men and boys who have been sexually assaulted or abused, may face additional barriers to resources (see 'T' for **Toxic Masculinity**). Stereotypes, homophobia, rigid gender roles, and the pervasive rape culture can make it hard for male survivors to disclose a sexual assault to friends, family, or the community. "Male victims may also have a hard time being believed, especially, if the assault was perpetrated by a woman. Some men who have survived sexual assault as adults feel shame or self-doubt, believing that they should have been 'strong enough' to fight off the perpetrator."[62] Male survivors who experience normal physiological responses to sexual stimulation such as an erection are confused by their bodies' response. No matter how a person's body responds to a sexual assault, it is never the victim's fault.[63] According to the Department of Justice:

o   As of 1998, 2.78 million men in the U.S. had been victims of attempted or completed rape.

o   About 3% of American men—or 1 in 33—have experienced an attempted or completed rape in their lifetime.

o   1 out of every 10 rape victims are male.[64]

•   **#METOO** is the hashtag that refers to *The MeToo Movement*™. The rallying cry "Me Too", was created by Tarana Burke, founder and director of Just Be, Inc. According to her website, the movement was created "to give young women, particularly young women of color from low wealth communities, a sense of empowerment from the understanding that they are not alone in their circumstances." [65] Burke founded the METOO movement in response to her work within these communities.

> *The position of the Just Be, Inc. organization, is that young women from low wealth backgrounds run the risk of being left feeling voiceless when they don't see themselves properly represented by various advocate groups, (see 'I' for **Intersectional feminism**, and 'W' for **Women of Color**). The me too Movement™[66] seeks to fill in those gaps and remove cultural barriers to resources for help and healing. Even as traumatic as sexual abuse, assault or exploitation is, sometimes there is nothing as powerful as knowing that you are not alone. The sooner young women understand that they are not an anomaly, the sooner they can begin their healing process. This is at the heart of **The me too Movement**™.[67]*

Although METOO was created by Burke in 2006, in 2017, actress Alyssa Milano used the #metoo as a show of solidarity with survivors of sexual assault amid sexual assault allegations against prominent Hollywood producer, Harvey Weinstein. At that time, she did not credit Tarana Burke for founding the me too Movement.[68] This prompted renewed conversations regarding the lack of attention surrounding the experiences of sexual assault experienced by **Women of Color** (see 'W'). See also "I for **Intersectional Feminism.**

•   **Military Sexual Trauma (MST)** is a term that includes both military sexual assault (MSA) and military sexual harassment (MSH). MST captures this spectrum of experiences, defined as "psychological trauma, which in the judgment of a….mental health professional, resulted from a physical assault of sexual nature, battery of a sexual nature, or sexual harassment which occurred while the Veteran was serving on active duty, active duty for training, or inactive duty training."[69] Awareness of the epidemic of sexual violence within the U.S. Armed Forces has grown over the past two-and-a-half decades. MST is currently recognized as a far-reaching problem that necessitates intervention. [70] Despite efforts to address the depth of MST, sexual violence in the military often goes unreported (see 'U' for **Under-reported**). According to the Department of Defense:

o   *18,900 military members experienced unwanted sexual contact in the fiscal year ending September, 2014*

o   *4.3% of active duty women and 0.9% of active duty men experienced unwanted sexual contact in FY14*

o *Of the 18,900 survivors, 43% of females and 10% of males reported*
o *Almost half of all Veterans who report MST are men* [71]

N is for:

- **"NO MEANS NO"** (see 'C' for *Consent*).

- **Non-Verbal Therapeutic Approaches** are promising models for healing sexual assault related post-traumatic stress. There are many paths to *Healing* (see 'H') from the trauma of sexual assault, and many options to address the psychological effects of sexual assault in addition to talk-based therapies. According to Kolk, in order to heal, "traumatic memories need to be transformed, contextualized, and given meaning, but words alone may be inadequate for addressing the negative imprint of trauma. "[72] By engaging in some newer therapeutic interventions, sexual assault survivors may identify traumatic memories, and integrate them. "Body-based therapies like *Yoga* (see 'Y'), eye movement Desensitization and Reprocessing (EMDR), neuro-feedback, and mindfulness meditation are among the recommended practices now utilized to keep the mind, brain, and body fully engaged in the present rather than trapped in the traumatic past."[73] In addition, creative arts therapies can help survivors of sexual assault access expression without the use of words. Van der Kolk explains, "the capacity for art, music, and dance to circumvent the speechlessness that comes with terror may be one reason they are used as trauma treatments in cultures around the world."[74] See also, "A" for *Art Therapy*, and "D" for *Dance Movement Therapy*.

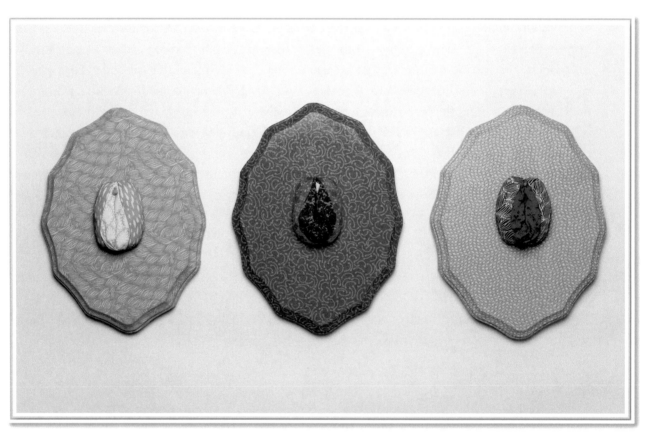

Jordan Ferranto, *Cunt*, Cotton fabric, thread, fiber fill, wooden trophy plagues, 2017

O is for:

- **Orders of protection** are civil orders issued by a judge to prevent one person from committing certain acts against others.

   The personal relationship between the 'respondent' (person alleged to commit the prohibited act) and the victim (person to be protected) determines which kind of petition would be filed. A protective order is a method to help keep a victim of family abuse or stalking safe from further acts of violence or stalking. A permanent protective order will usually only be issued after a full hearing before the appropriate court."[75]

   Each state has different restraining order laws that lay out the requirements for getting an order of protection. An order of protection does not guarantee safety. Some examples of orders of protection are:

   o   Stalking No Contact Order
   o   Domestic violence order of protection
   o   Sexual Assault- Civil No Contact Order: "Similar to a domestic violence order of protection, a civil no contact order is a court order that can protect a survivor and their family or household members from an abuser if they are the victim of non-consensual sexual conduct or non-consensual sexual penetration. Unlike the domestic violence order of protection, a survivor does not need to have a specific relationship with the abuser to get a civil no contact order."[76] *Legal advocates* (see 'L') can help survivors file the correct paperwork at the courthouse and petition for orders of contact.

P is for:

- **Perpetrator** is the legal term used to reference a person accused of sexual assault. Perpetrators of rape are often serial criminals. According to recent statistics, out of 1000 Perpetrators referred to prosecutors:

   o   *370 have at least one prior felony conviction, including 100 who have 5 or more*
   o   *520 will be released—either because they posted bail or for other reasons—while awaiting trial*
   o   *70 of the released perpetrators will be arrested for committing another crime before their case is decided.*[77]

   It is important to note that the imprisonment of sex offenders is a "poor substitute for substantive and transformative social change."[78] Despite evidence that penal measures do not necessarily keep communities safe from sexual violence, incarceration is one of the only options for containing sexual predators. A more substantive long-term solution to address the epidemic of sexual violence is needed. Although the 1990's saw an effort to monitor sexual predators through sex offender registries, surveillance of sex offenders, does not keep communities safe from sexual violence.[79] See also, "J" for *Justice???*

- **Post-traumatic Stress Disorder (PTSD)** is a diagnosis that describes a cluster of symptoms that a person may experience as a result of either directly experiencing or witnessing traumatic events. A diagnosis may be given to a person in a medical setting as a way of categorizing and justifying the treatment for the symptoms the traumatized person is experiencing. Some people may find a diagnosis of PTSD to be stigmatizing and possibly harmful. While addressing the trauma of sexual assault, some people prefer to use the term "*Rape Trauma Syndrome*" (see 'R') to describe the symptoms a person experiences during and after an act of sexual violence. The Diagnostic and Statistical Manual of Mental Disorders (DSM-V), lists the criteria for a diagnosis of PTSD under *Trauma- and Stressor-Related Disorders*. A person may receive a diagnosis of PTSD after a sexual assault that they experienced directly, or witnessed if in the aftermath of the assault, they re-experience the trauma during nightmares and flashbacks. There are other key symptoms of PTSD, including feeling isolated, irritable, aggressive, negative, hyper vigilant, having difficulty recalling key features of the trauma, difficulty concentrating, or sleeping. [80]

Q is for:

- **Queer Survivorship** is a term used to describe people who identify within the Queer community who have experienced sexual assault. According to the Centers for Disease Control and Prevention (CDC), "people who identify as lesbian, gay and bisexual experience sexual violence at similar or higher rates than heterosexuals." [81] The "National Coalition of Anti-Violence Projects estimates that nearly one in ten LGBTQ survivors of intimate partner violence (IPV) has experienced sexual assault from those partners. Studies suggest that around half of transgender people and bisexual women will experience sexual violence at some point in their lifetimes." [82] In addition, "within the LGBTQ community, transgender people and bisexual women face the most alarming rates of sexual violence. Among both of these populations, sexual violence begins early, often during childhood. The 2015 U.S. Transgender Survey found that 47% of transgender people are sexually assaulted at some point in their lifetime," according to the CDC's National Intimate Partner and Sexual Violence Survey. [83] People in the LGBTQ community often face a variety of challenges that add layers to their *Intersectional* (see 'I'), identities. Those that identify within this community have "higher rates of poverty, stigma, and marginalization, which put them at greater risk for sexual assault, and the symptoms associated with PTSD." [84] They also face higher rates of hate-motivated violence, (see 'I' for *Incarceration and Sexual Assault* and *Intersectional Feminsim,* and 'X' for *Xenephobia*), which can often take the form of sexual assault. People in the LGBTQ community often encounter discrimination in response to their identities, which can make them reluctant to seek resources for healing within institutions and systems that may further exacerbate their trauma. [85]

Mikey Anderson, *Untitled #1and #2,* Embroidery floss and found fabric, 2018

R is for:

- **Rape Trauma Syndrome** (RTS) is the medical term given to the response that most survivors have to the experience of being raped. "It is very important to note that RTS is the natural response of a psychologically healthy person to the trauma of rape so these symptoms do not constitute a mental disorder or illness."[86] Within RTS, the clusters of reactions to sexual assault have been organized into three stages: an acute immediate phase of disruption and disorganization, a long-term process of reorganization, and another phase known as the "underground" phase. RTS is made up of clusters of physical, behavioral, and psychological symptoms that may manifest immediately or over a period of time. Every person has their own unique response to the trauma of sexual assault, and while most survivors will experience a variety of symptoms categorized as RTS, some survivors may only experience a few of these symptoms or none at all. "It is important not to judge whether someone has been raped, by the number of symptoms that they display."[87] Because of the enduring *Rape Culture* (see 'R'), that permeates society; the myths, biases, and stigma associated with rape can exacerbate a survivor's trauma. Cultural attitudes can add to the overall burden a survivor may endure.[88] See also "A" for *Ally*, "B" for *Believe Survivors*, "I" for *It's Not Your Fault*, and "V" for *Victim Blaming*.

- **Rape** is a nonconsensual sex act. Although, it is important to note that the act of raping someone is not only about sex, but the use of sexual acts to dominate and overpower the person being assaulted. The specific use of sexual acts to overpower and degrade another person violates the most intimate and vulnerable parts of that person. The violent act of rape produces a psychological trauma, comparable only to the combat of war. See 'P' for *Post-traumatic Stress Disorder.* [89]

- **Rape culture:** The sociological and cultural theory of *Rape Culture* originated in the 1970s during the rise of second-wave feminism. Theorists broadly define rape culture as "an all-encompassing belief system that supports or excuses sexual harassment and assault."[90] Factors such as traditional gender roles, sexual beliefs, and acceptance of interpersonal violence were identified as the foundations of a rape culture. Rape culture thrives due to rigid gender roles enforced within a society that "socializes boys to be sexual aggressors and girls to be sexually passive. Further more, rape culture theorists find sexism is related to rape and sexual assault as it maintains the imbalance of power between men and women, limiting women's ability to have their voices heard both figuratively through **Victim Blaming** (see 'V'), and literally through ignoring the word 'no.' (see 'N' for **No Means No**)."[91] See also "Z" for **Zero Tolerance**.

- A **Rape Kit**, (also called a *Sexual Assault Evidence Kit* (SAEK)), is a container that includes a checklist, materials, and instructions, along with envelopes and containers to package any specimens collected during a sexual assault forensics exam. A person who has experienced a sexual assault may choose to go to the emergency room to receive a thorough physical examination, as well as have DNA evidence collected from their body, clothes, and other personal belongings by a *Sexual Assault Nurse Examiner* (SANE) — a registered nurse who has received specialized education and fulfilled clinical requirements to perform the exam. Many hospital emergency rooms have SANE trained nurses on staff. In most cases, DNA evidence needs to be collected within 72 hours of the assault in order to be analyzed by a crime lab. Although it is not required that a person reports the sexual assault in order to have an exam, the process of collecting evidence does allow the person the chance to safely store evidence should they decide to report at a later time. The amount of time an evidence kit will be stored varies by state and jurisdiction.[92] When a person discloses a sexual assault at a hospital, hospital staff may also call a rape victim advocate (see 'V' for **Volunteer**), to come to the ER. Medical advocates are trained volunteers that help rape victims navigate the rape kit process while informing them of their rights and acting as liaisons between medical and law enforcement personnel.

- **Resilience** is *1: the capability of a strained body to recover its size and shape after deformation caused especially by compressive stress **2:** an ability to recover from or adjust easily to misfortune or change* [93]

When referring to sexual assault, the term resilience is used to describe the ability of sexual assault victims to evolve into sexual assault survivors. The path to recovery may not be linear, and the work may be challenging, but human beings are incredibly resilient, and with the right support and attention, it is possible to begin the **Healing** (see 'H') process after experiencing sexual assault. There are rape crisis centers, counseling services, and resources dedicated to survivors of sexual assault and their allies.

S is for:

- **Sexual Assault** is defined differently from state to state. According to the Justice Department, The legal definition of sexual assault encompasses "any nonconsensual (see 'C' for **Consent**) sexual act proscribed by Federal, tribal, or State law, including when the victim lacks capacity to consent."[94] Some states define sexual assault as any nonconsensual act of vaginal, oral, or anal *penetration*. If a rapist is convicted, sexual assault is generally a felony offense.[95] Different terms are used when referring to legal definitions and specific acts of sexual violence, and each state uses different terms, ranging from sexual assault, to rape, to sexual battery. The Rape and Incest National Network has a *State Law Database* at https://apps.rainn.org/policy/ that details how each state defines sexual assault.[96]

- **Sex Workers** are people who receive money or goods in exchange for sexual services. "Sex work is any type of labor where the explicit goal is to produce a sexual or erotic response in the client. Sex work includes prostitution, but it also describes other forms of work like erotic dancing, webcam work, sensual massage, adult film, phone sex, etc."[97] The "institutional alienation of sex workers from law enforcement protection," leaves sex workers vulnerable to sexual assault. According to Sex Workers Outreach Project, (SWOP) "most interactions between sex workers and law enforcement involve the arrest of sex workers, and law enforcement and judicial system officials frequently ignore or doubt reports of sexual assault made by sex workers."[98] Sex workers rarely report sexual and physical assaults to law enforcement because of their distrust of the legal system, which makes them more vulnerable to sexual violence. Those who want to learn more can visit Sex Workers Outreach Project at www.swopusa.org, and also see "I" for **Intersectional Feminism**.

- **Survivor** is used as a term of empowerment to describe someone who has experienced sexual assault. Both the label "victim" and "survivor" are used to describe persons that have experienced sexual assault, and both are applicable. Medical professionals and Law enforcement officials use the word victim when referring to someone who has recently been affected by sexual violence; or when referring to a specific crime or case against a perpetrator. The word survivor is often used to refer to someone who is going through the recovery process, or when discussing the short- or long-term effects of sexual violence. Some people use the word survivor as a way of reclaiming power and agency after they have experienced assault. Some people identify as victims, while others prefer the term survivor. It is important to let the person who experienced the assault, define themselves in the way in which they choose to be defined, and to respect and support their decision.[99]

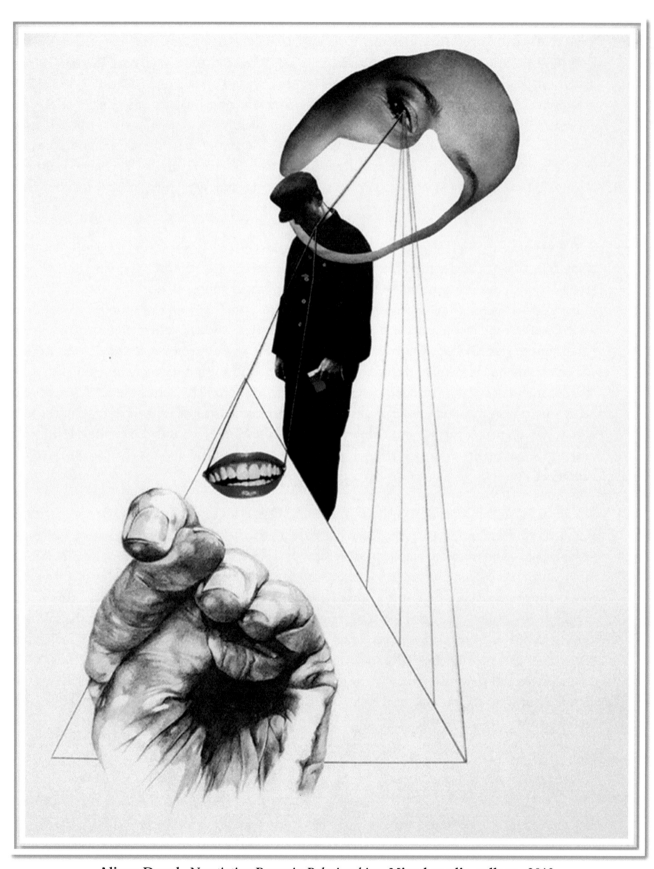

Alison Dowd, *Negotiating Power in Relationships***, Mixed media collage, 2013**

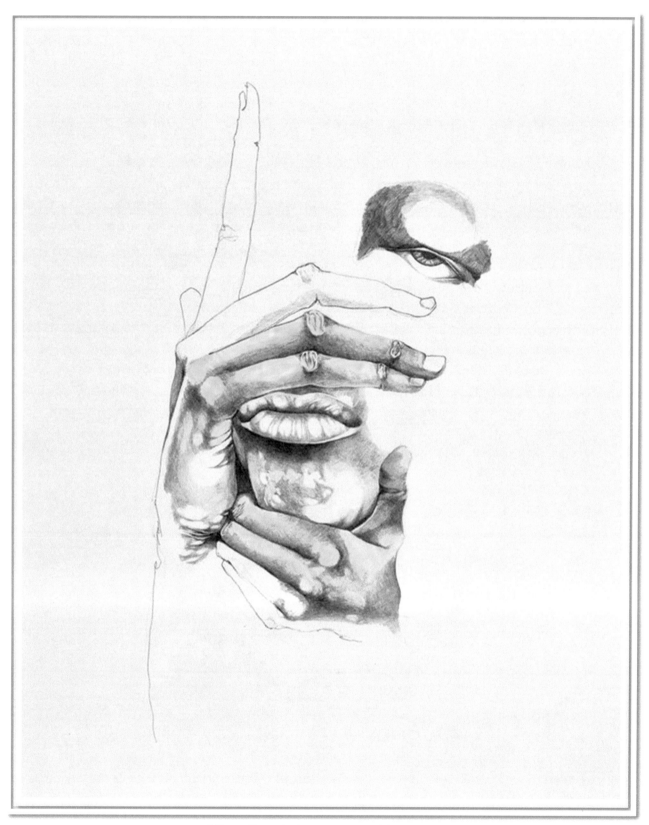

Alison Dowd, *Survivor*, **Graphite, 2015**

T is for:

- **Toxic Masculinity** [100] is a term that is used to describe "a narrow and repressive description of manhood, as defined by violence, sex, status, and aggression."[101] Others define toxic masculinity as "a specific model of manhood, geared toward dominance and control."[102] Some argue that socially constructed gender binaries that prescribe inherently "masculine" and "feminine" behavior, is the true source of this toxicity.[103] The concept of toxic masculinity seems to be closely related to, or perhaps a foundation for, **Rape Culture** (see 'R'). See also "V", for **Victim Blaming**.

- Human Sex **Trafficking** is defined as "the induction of a person by force, fraud, or coercion to participate in commercial sex acts, or in which the person induced to perform such act(s) has not attained 18 years of age. Human Trafficking/Involuntary Servitude is the obtaining of a person(s) through recruitment, harboring, transportation, or provision, and subjecting such persons by force, fraud, or coercion into involuntary servitude, peonage, debt bondage, or slavery (not to include commercial sex acts)."[104] Sex Trafficking is not to be confused with **Sex Work** (see 'S'), which is the consensual exchange of sexual acts for goods or services performed by a **Sex Worker** (see 'C' for **Consent**). Sex trafficking has devastating consequences for the trafficked individual. If victims of trafficking are detained by law enforcement, they may face criminal prosecution for prostitution. In addition, victims may suffer from long-lasting physical and psychological trauma (see 'P' for **PTSD**), disease (HIV/AIDS), drug addiction, malnutrition and social ostracism. The National Human Trafficking Hotline is: **1 (888) 373-7888**. [105]

- **Trauma**
  Trauma is the Greek word for "wound". Although the Greeks used the term to refer to physical injuries, nowadays the word *trauma* also refers to psychological wounds. A *traumatic* event such as a sexual assault, can manifest psychological symptoms long after any physical injuries have healed. **Post-Traumatic Stress Disorder**, or **PTSD** (see 'P'), is the clinical name used to describe the residual psychological reactions to both physical and emotional trauma. See also, "R" for **Rape Trauma Syndrome**.

- A **Trigger** is defined as *a: to release or activate by means of a trigger*
             b: to cause the explosion of
             2: to initiate, actuate, or set off by a trigger[106]

When describing symptoms related to **PTSD** (See 'P') or **Rape Trauma Syndrome**, the word trigger refers to a reminder of the past trauma that sets off a neurological reaction that could lead to flashbacks, dissociative episodes, anxiety attacks, or any combination of these symptoms where the person being "triggered" is reliving the danger and associated physiological responses they experienced during the original trauma. A trigger could be anything that even vaguely reminds the person of the trauma, even unconsciously, such as the scent of someone's cologne, a song on the radio, or a particular street corner. A person in a "triggered" state may feel like they are re-living the traumatic event, and may not be able to cognitively understand that they are not *presently* in danger. **Grounding Techniques** (see 'G') and conscious **Breathing** (see 'B') may be employed to calm the sympathetic nervous system, of a person who is triggered. For more information, see 'F' for *Flight, Fight, or Freeze*.

U is for:

- Sexual assault is woefully **Under- Reported**. Sexual violence is often referred to as a *silent epidemic,* due to the high rate of assaults in contrast to the low rate of reporting. According to the Department of Justice, only 310 out of every 1,000 sexual assaults are reported to police. That translates into 2 out of 3 sexual assaults going unreported.[107] The reason for this silence is in relation to a culture that often condones, or turns a blind eye to sexual assault, or blames the victim for their assault (see 'R' for *Rape Culture* and 'V' for *Victim Blaming*). There are many reasons why a survivor may not report a sexual assault, (see 'B' for *Believe Survivors*). Women surveyed by the department of justice, gave these reasons for not reporting:

In general:

- 20% feared retaliation
- 13% believed the police would not do anything to help
- 13% believed it was a personal matter
- 8% reported to a different official
- 8% believed it was not important enough to report
- 7% did not want to get the perpetrator in trouble
- 2% believed the police could not do anything to help
- 30% gave another reason, or did not cite one reason

Among individuals of college-age[108]

- o Female Students: 20% report
- o Female Non-Students: 32% report

Among the elderly:

- o 28% report[109]

Among members of the military:

- o 43% of female victims and 10% of male victims reported.[110]

Robert Narciso, *Home, Home?*, Paint and oil pastel on paper, 2017

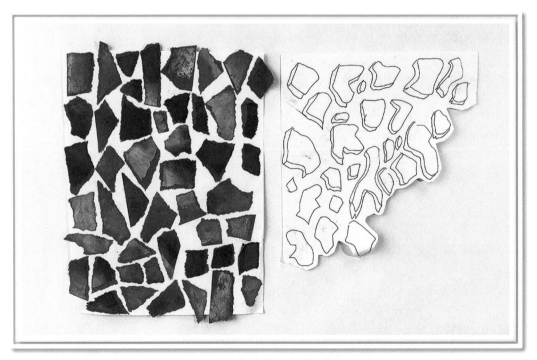

Robert Narciso, *Deconstructed*, Paint and oil pastel on paper, 2018

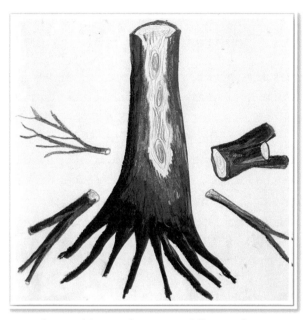

Robert Nacriso, *A Tree in the Forest,* **Oil pastel on paper, 2018**

V is for:

- **Vicarious Trauma** refers to the experience of symptoms that resemble *Post Traumatic Stress*, as a result of being in proximity to trauma. People who witness sexual violence or hold space for someone recovering from the trauma of a sexual assault, may experience vicarious trauma. This can happen to allies, friends, family members, first responders, health-care workers, those working in the criminal justice system, and communities at large. The trauma of sexual violence can affect anyone who comes into contact with it, even on an unconscious level. Allies that support victims in the aftermath of an assault may experience symptoms such as nightmares, anxiety, and hyper-vigilance as a result of the stories they bear witness to. It is important that those who support or work directly with survivors of sexual assault, also find ways of processing the trauma they encounter, through support groups, community care, counseling, and other therapeutic modalities.[111]

- **Victim Blaming** is "a devaluing act where the victim of a crime, an accident, or any type of abusive maltreatment is held as wholly or partially responsible for the wrongful conduct committed against them. Victim blaming can appear in the form of negative social reactions from legal, medical, and mental health professionals, as well as from the media, immediate family members, and other acquaintances. Misconceptions about victims, perpetrators, and the nature of sexual violence can also contribute to victim blaming. Victims sometimes blame themselves and internalize the shame and anger they experience as a result of the assault. Victim blaming, may also be the direct result of being victimized while living within a dominant *Rape Culture,* (see 'R'). Blame for sexual violence can be attributed to a widespread cultural attitude that condones the violence towards, and domination of, women and marginalized communities. There is no activity, clothing item, or amount of drinks that a victim has had that justifies the violent act of sexual assault. Sexual assault is a felony crime, and the perpetrator who committed the assault, and the society that permits them to, are to blame. See also "I" for "*It's Not Your Fault*."[112]

- A rape crisis **Volunteer** is someone who may provide support for a sexual assault survivor in a variety of roles. Volunteers may act as a medical advocate, meeting survivors in emergency rooms to inform them of their rights and be by their side if they decide to participate in a rape kit. Volunteers may answer the phone at a hotline. Volunteers may provide legal advocacy or educational and outreach services for survivors and their allies. There are currently hundreds of rape crisis centers located nationally that rely heavily upon the support of volunteers. There are national organizations and independent sexual assault service providers, dedicated to helping survivors at the local level. Volunteering for a local rape crisis center is one way to support survivors and combat sexual violence in an impactful way (see 'A' for *Ally* and 'C' for *Community and Connection*). [113] Local volunteer opportunities are detailed at https://volopps.rainn.org/.

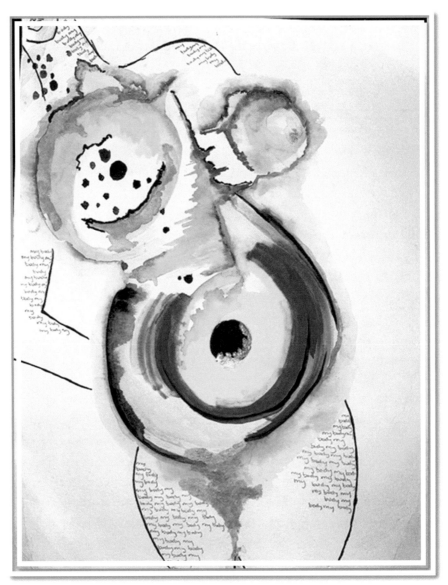

Toni Eldimere, *My Body*, graphite pencil, acrylic paint pens, watercolor on mixed media paper, 2019

W is for:

- **Women of Color** are particularly susceptible to sexual violence at the oppressive intersection of sexism and racism, (see 'I' for **Intersectional Feminism**). Institutionalized racism often creates barriers for Women of Color to access support. Women of color may find it difficult to trust the systems and institutions that tend to minimize or criminalize their experiences. There may be language or cultural barriers that make it hard for Women of Color, and immigrant women in particular, to disclose abuse. Immigrant status may also deter survivors from coming forward to disclose sexual assault. Women of Color may feel like disclosing sexual assault would be a betrayal to their communities.[114] Among women of color, Indigenous women are at the greatest risk of sexual violence. "On average, American Indians ages 12 and older experience 5,900 sexual assaults per year."[115] It is imperative that the experiences and voices of women of color are centered, within the **Anti-Rape Movement** (see 'A'), in order to address the needs of the most marginalized survivors of sexual assault. See also "M" for **The Me Too Movement** and "X" for **Xenephobia**.

Rochele Royster, *Judith's Redemption: The Death of Holofernes,* **Oil on canvas, 2015**

X is for:

- **Xenephobia** *is*: "The fear and hatred of strangers or foreigners or of anything that is strange or foreign."[116] Xenophobia and sexual violence can intersect violently, when experienced by people who are foreign. "Nationally and internationally, xenophobia has the political face of exclusion or inclusion and access to resources. Immigrants and refugees have very little recourse, and little access to resources when it comes to sexual violence. Often times, it is clear that sexual violence perpetrated against foreigners, has the attributes of a hate crime". Foreign people who experience sexual violence without citizenship status, are some of the most vulnerable to the complex trauma that may follow a sexual assault. [117] See also 'W' for **Women of Color**, and 'I' for **Intersectional Feminism**.

Y is for:

- **Yoga** is a promising therapeutic approach for post trauma symptoms. Because yoga is body-oriented (see 'E' for **Embodied**), People who have participated in yoga have reported an improvement in body awareness. By utilizing physical stretching poses, yoga allows a person to slowly and deliberately embrace their physicality in a safe and controlled way. Yoga is structured but also emphasizes choice. Yoga practice facilitates opportunities for deep breathing (see 'B' for **Breathe** and 'G' for **Grounding**), and a connection to the natural rhythms of the body. Through breath work and meditation associated with yoga, mindfulness can be cultivated, which addresses many symptoms associated with **PTSD** (see 'P') such as **Dissociation** (see 'D') and anxiety.[118] Many community centers and local park districts offer access to yoga classes for all levels of students. In addition, there are a variety of yoga tutorials streaming online for free.

Z is for:

- **Zero tolerance** refers to a disallowance of words, actions, or deeds that contribute to **Rape Culture** and all forms of *acceptable aggression* towards women and marginalized communities. Committing to a *zero tolerance* attitude, means creating safe environments for all people to exist, free from sexist jokes, harassment, and sexual violence. Employing a *zero tolerance* standard towards behavior that contributes to the **Rape Culture** (see 'R'), means speaking up and out against all forms of sexism, homophobia, transphobia, and gender-based violence. One may do this by calling in friends, family, and institutions to engage in meaningful dialogue surrounding the concepts of **Victim Blaming** (see 'V'), and **Rape Culture** (see 'R'). See also "N" for **No Means no.**

ARTISTS FEATURED

Mikey Anderson, LCPC, ATR is a Queer crafter from the south side of Chicago. His crafts are informed by his community-driven art therapy practice that intersects between art, art therapy, Queer theory, and activism.

Neha Bhat is an artist, feminist and art therapist that works bi-culturally. from a trauma-informed, attachment-oriented lens and is interested in a conjunction of social justice, trauma-therapy, art and mysticism. www.nehabhat.org

Annie Chang's identity as a second-generation Korean American woman simultaneously informs her practice as a visual artist and art therapist. She creates installations and sculptural garments while utilizing photography and writing to document her experiences with oppression as a form of politicized active participation and as a means to personally dissect intersectionality. She incorporates imagery and symbols which relate to her cultural heritage and lineage, relationships, personal experiences, and reflect upon the performance of identity and levels of transparency. The relationship of objects and spaces relate to her view of people and the places and systems they inhabit.

Trissa Dodson, LCPC, LMHC, ATR is a licensed counselor and art therapist, as well as a practicing artist. She received a Master of Art in Art Therapy and Counseling from the School of the Art Institute of Chicago. She is currently based in Orlando, FL and provides trauma therapy to people throughout Florida and Illinois. Trissa mainly works with clients who have experienced trauma, particularly sexual assault or child sexual abuse. Using a blend of art therapy, sex therapy, traditional talk therapy, and EMDR (Eye Movement Desensitization and Reprocessing), she helps people process issues with PTSD, anxiety, low self-esteem, body-awareness, relationships, sex/intimacy, sexuality, and identity. Trissa's art practice ranges from creating as a means of processing personal responses to therapeutic content; reflecting on personal themes like vulnerability, feminism, and intimacy; raising public awareness on issues; or simply as a means of playing and exploring new materials.

Alison Dowd, LCPC, is an artist in Chicago, Il whose work explores themes of identity, relationships and conflict that oscillate between interpersonal and political domains. Her understanding of art therapy is rooted in arts activism, critical pedagogy, and community practice. www.allisondowd.com

Toni Eldemire, LCPC, ATR is a Licensed Clinical Professional Counselor, Artist, and Art Therapist in Chicago. Toni is the founder of One Love Studio, where she provides a safe therapeutic space for people to explore their relationship to self, others, and the systems we participate in. Toni connects, mirrors, and encourages individuals to tear down their walls of self-doubt with curiosity, love and compassion. Her therapeutic work as an art therapist is informed by a cultural – relational, feminist, narrative, trauma – informed approach with a social justice lens. She believes artmaking to be a way to externalize oppression, call out injustice and promote the healing process. Her art making is centered around human emotions. Through nontraditional self-portraits and journal entries, I explore my own identity in order to develop a connection with the viewer. https://www.onelovestudio.org/

Beth Enterkin, LCPC, is an artist and art therapist who has dedicated her career to the healing of trauma, especially domestic violence and sexual assault. Beth uses her own artwork to better understand and empathize with her clients, to heal herself from the vicarious trauma of her work, and to educate others about the impacts of interpersonal trauma and fight against the stigma placed on survivors.

Jordan Ferranto, LCPC, ATR is a sex therapist and art therapist in private practice. She conceptualizes the therapeutic process as the intentional application of curiosity and attention. She invites her clients to develop an experimental mindset as a way to enter into deeper understandings of themselves. Establishing an authentic and unwavering relationship with oneself is the foundation of her work with clients as they explore their definitions of sexual and relational wellness.

Christina Heyworth, MAATC, ATR-P (she/her) is a Chicago based visual artist and graphic medicine author. Her current praxis involves themes of memory, community, and ecopsychotherapy. She held art therapy internships with JourneyCare and ABBHH before graduating from The School of the Art Institute's Master of Art in Art Therapy program in 2021.

Catherine Moon, is Professor Emeritus of the Art Therapy Department at the School of the Art Institute of Chicago. She is an artist, author, and the co-facilitator of therapeutic arts trainings in East Africa.

Robert Narciso, LCPC is an artist and art therapist living and working in Chicago Il. Art impacts processing and allows people to move forward with more creative insight. The artworks created for this publication were created while facilitating expressive therapy groups at an adult psychiatric hospital. @ badlittlerobbie

Annie Novotny, LCPC, ATR Annie Novotny is an artist, art therapist, educator, and a survivor. She facilitates art therapy and trauma counseling with individuals, couples, and groups within her private practice **Roots and Rays Creative Counseling** on Chicago's Southwest side. Annie is a professor at The School of the Art Institute of Chicago, attends to her own art practice, and mothers two young girls. Annie felt moved to create this text while working with Veterans with Military Sexual Trauma histories and sexual assault survivors- to serve as a tool to support and empower their recovery and healing process. www.rootsandrayscounseling.com

Patrick Morrissey—LCPC, ATR received his Master of Arts in Art Therapy from the School of the Art Institute of Chicago in 2005. He currently works as a Creative Arts Therapist at the Jesse Brown VA Medical Center in Chicago. As the first art therapist employed at JBVA, Mr. Morrissey initiated a creative arts therapy program to provide group and individual art therapy to a diverse population of veterans emphasizing clinical work with complex trauma including PTSD, Moral Injury, and Military Sexual Trauma.

Rochele Royster, PHD, ATR-BC, is an artist, art therapist and educator. She has worked for the last 20 years integrating art therapy into the general education curriculum for diverse learners in Chicago Public Schools on the South and West Sides of Chicago She is a professor in the art therapy department at Syracuse University, College of Visual and Performing Arts.

Farah Salem is a visual artist, activist, and art therapist from Kuwait and is currently based in Chicago. The underlying motif for her artwork is to capture raw human emotions, questioning ways of erasing socio-cultural conditioning, and challenging systems of oppression.

Teresa "T". Sit, LCPC, is an Art Therapist and Licensed Clinical Professional Counselor who specializes in supporting survivors of trauma. Born and raised in the south suburbs of Chicago, T. was inspired to become a therapist by her community and her mom, Kim, a survivor whose parenting journey was dedicated to ending the cycle of abuse in their family. T holds a BFA in Photography from UIUC (2002) and a MAAT from SAIC (2017).

Danyah Subei, MAATC, LAC, ATR, Danyah received a Master of Arts in Art Therapy and Counseling from the School of the Art Institute of Chicago and is a Registered Art Therapist. She is certified through the Arizona Board of Behavioral Health as a Licensed Associate Counselor and is working to become a Licensed Professional Counselor.

ENDNOTES

1   Ally. (n.d.). Retrieved from https://www.merriam- webster.com/dictionary/ally?utm_campaign=sd&utm_medium=serp&utm_source=jsonld

2   Taylor, S. R. (2018, April 17). Here are 9 Ways To Be A Good Ally To Sexual Assault Survivors. Retrieved from https://thebodyisnotanapology.com/magazine/here-are-9-ways-to-be-a-good-ally-to-sexual-assault-survivors

3   (n.d.). Retrieved from https://www.rainn.org/articles/help-someone-you-care-about

4   Illinois Coalition Against Sexual Assault: English: Home. (n.d.). Retrieved from http://www.icasa.org/

5   History of the Rape Crisis Movement. (2009, November 17). Retrieved from http://www.calcasa.org/2009/11/history-of-the-rape-crisis-movement/

6   Lerner, G. (1992). *Black women in white America: A documentary history*. New York: Vintage Books.
    Feimster, C. N. (2018, February 02). How Formerly Enslaved Black Women Fought for Sexual Justice. Retrieved from https://slate.com/human-interest/2018/02/how-formerly-enslaved-black-women-fought-for-human-dignity-and-sexual-justice.html

7   History of the Rape Crisis Movement. (2009, November 17). Retrieved from http://www.calcasa.org/2009/11/history-of-the-rape-crisis-movement/

8   American Art Therapy Association. (n.d.). Retrieved from https://arttherapy.org/

9   Talwar, S. (2007). Accessing traumatic memory through art making: An art therapy trauma protocol (ATTP). *The Arts in Psychotheapy*, 34(1), 22-35. doi: 10.1016/j.aip.2006.09.001

10 Tripp, T. (2016). A Body-Based Bilateral Art Protocol for Reprocessing Trauma. In J. L. King (Ed.), *Art therapy, trauma and neuroscience: Theoretical and practical perspectives*. Basingstoke: Taylor & Francis. (p. 174)

11 #believesurvivors, #Ibelieveyou, #believewomen

12 Me too. Movement. (n.d.). Retrieved from https://metoomvmt.org/

13 Seppala, E., Abadilla, N., & Hansen, A. J. (2018, January 23). The remarkable impact of yoga breathing for trauma. Retrieved from https://scopeblog.stanford.edu/2014/01/31/the-remarkable-impact-of-yoga-breathing-for-trauma

14 Kolk, B. A. (2015). *The body keeps the score: Mind, brain and body in the transformation of trauma*. London: Penguin Books. (p. 79)

15 Consent. (n.d.). Retrieved from https://www.merriam-webster.com/dictionary/consent?utm_campaign=sd&utm_medium=serp&utm_source=jsonld

16 Planned Parenthood. (n.d.). What Is Sexual Consent? / Facts About Rape & Sexual Assault. Retrieved from https://www.plannedparenthood.org/learn/sex-and-relationships/sexual-consent

17 Kolk, B. A. (2015). *The body keeps the score: Mind, brain and body in the transformation of trauma*. London: Penguin Books. (p. 212)

18 American Dance Therapy Association. (n.d.). Retrieved from https://adta.org

19 Kolk, B. A. (2015). *The body keeps the score: Mind, brain and body in the transformation of trauma*. London: Penguin Books. (p. 240)

20 (n.d.). Retrieved from https://www.rainn.org/statistics/perpetrators-sexual-violence

21 (n.d.). Retrieved from https://www.rainn.org/articles/sexual-abuse-people-disabilities

22 http://www.icasa.org/index.aspx?pageid=1044

23 https://www.bjs.gov/content/pub/pdf/capd10st.pdf

24 https://www.rainn.org/articles/sexual-abuse-people-disabilities

25 Porges, S. W. (2017). *The pocket guide to the polyvagal theory: The transformative power of feeling safe*. New York: W.W. Norton.

26 Porges, S. W. (2017). *The pocket guide to the polyvagal theory: The transformative power of feeling safe*. New York: W.W. Norton.

27 NCADV | National Coalition Against Domestic Violence. (n.d.). Retrieved from https://ncadv.org/learn-more

28 https://www.womenshealth.gov/a-z-topics/date-rape-drugs

29 http://www.idph.state.il.us/about/womenshealth/factsheets/date.htm

30 https://www.merriam-webster.com/dictionary/embodied?utm_campaign=sd&utm_medium=serp&utm_source=jsonld

31 Kolk, B. A. (2015). *The body keeps the score: Mind, brain and body in the transformation of trauma*. London: Penguin Books. (P. 99)

32 https://www.merriam-webster.com/dictionary/empathy

33 Brown, B. (2008). *I thought it was just me (but it isnt): Making the Journey from "What Will People Think?" to "I Am Enough"*. New York: Avery.

34 Kolk, B. A. (2015). *The body keeps the score: Mind, brain and body in the transformation of trauma*. London: Penguin Books. (p. 79)

35 Kolk, B. A. (2015). *The body keeps the score: Mind, brain and body in the transformation of trauma*. London: Penguin Books. (p. 85)

36 Gantt, L., & Tinnin, L. W. (2009). Support for a neurobiological view of trauma with implications for art therapy. *The Arts in Psychotherapy*, 36(3), 148-153. Doi: 10.1016/j.aip.2008.12.005

37 https://www.petewalker.com

38 https://www.pete-walker.com/codependencyFawnResponse.html

39 https://www.sexualtraumacounsellingperth.com/single-post/2018/06/24/Using-Grounding-in-Trauma-Recovery

40 https://www.medicalnewstoday.com/articles/317098.php

41 https://www.rainn.org/articles/sexual-harassment

42 www.ourresilience.org, www.ywca.org

43 https://www.rainn.org/statistics/children-and-teens

44 Incest | RAINN. (n.d.). Retrieved from https://www.rainn.org/articles/incest

45 https://www.cdc.gov/violenceprevention/acestudy/index.html

46 https://www.rainn.org/statistics/children-and-teens
    1. H.M Zinzow, H.S. Resnick, J.L. McCauley, A.B. Amstadter, K.J. Ruggiero, & D.G. Kilpatrick, Prevalence and risk of psychiatric disorders as a function of variant rape histories: results from a national survey of women. Social psychiatry and psychiatric epidemiology, 47(6), 893-902 (2012).

47 https://siawso.wildapricot.org/

48 https://www.hrw.org/reports/2001/prison/report4.html

49 1. Department of Justice, Office of Justice Programs, Bureau of Justice Statistics, Sexual Victimization in Prisons and Jails Reported by Inmates, 2011-2012 (2013).

50 https://www.prearesourcecenter.org/about/prison-rape-elimination-act-prea

51 https://www.merriam-webster.com/dictionary/intersectionality?src=search-dict-box

52 Goodman, R. D., PhD, LPC. (2015). *A Liberatory Approach to Trauma Counseling: Decolonizing Our Trauma-Informed Practices*. 55-72. 10.1007/978-1-4939-1283-4_5.

53 https://www.fbi.gov/investigate/civil-rights/hate-crimes

54 https://www.merriam-webster.com/dictionary/justice

55 https://www.rainn.org/statistics/criminal-justice-system
    I.   Department of Justice, Office of Justice Programs, Bureau of Justice Statistics, National Crime Victimization Survey, 2010-2014 (2015);
    II. Federal Bureau of Investigation, National Incident-Based Reporting System, 2012-2014 (2015);
    III. Federal Bureau of Investigation, National Incident-Based Reporting System, 2012-2014 (2015);
    IV. Department of Justice, Office of Justice Programs, Bureau of Justice Statistics, Felony Defendants in Large Urban Counties, 2009 (2013).

56 1. Federal Bureau of Investigation, National Incident-Based Reporting System, 2012-2014 (2015); iv. Department of Justice, Office of Justice Programs, Bureau of Justice Statistics, Felony Defendants in Large Urban Counties, 2009 (2013).

57 http://icasa.org/forms.aspx?Pageid=591&SearchQuery=child%20sexual%20abuse

58 http://icasa.org/forms.aspx?Pageid=591&SearchQuery=child%20sexual%20abuse

59 1. https://www.rainn.org/statistics/children-and-teens
    2. United States Department of Health and Human Services, Administration for Children and Families, Administration on Children, Youth and Families, Children's Bureau. Child Maltreatment Survey, 2013 (2014).

60 National Institute of Justice. 2006. *Extent, Nature, and Consequences of Rape Victimization: Findings From the National Violence Against Women Survey.*

61 American Academy of Pediatrics. Committee on Adolescence. Sexual Assault and the Adolescent. 5 *Pediatrics.* (1994): 761-765.

62 https://www.rainn.org/articles/sexual-assault-men-and-boys

63 https://1in6.org/, https://www.rainn.org/articles/sexual-assault-men-and-boys

64 1. Department of Justice, Office of Justice Programs, Bureau of Justice Statistics, Female Victims of Sexual Violence, 1994-2010 (2013).
    2. https://www.rainn.org/statistics/victims-sexual-violence

65 http://justbeinc.wixsite.com/justbeinc/the-me-too-movement-c7cf

66 https://metoomvmt.org/

67 http://justbeinc.wixsite.com/justbeinc/the-me-too-movement-c7cf

68 https://www.nytimes.com/2017/10/20/us/me-too-movement-tarana-burke.html

69 Lofgreen, A. M., Carroll, K. K., Dugan, S. A., & Karnik, N. S. (2017). An Overview of Sexual Trauma in the U.S. Military. *Focus, 15*(4), 411-419. doi:10.1176/appi.focus.20170024

70 www.mentalhealth.va.gov/msthome.asp

71 1. Department of Defense, Fiscal Year 2014 Annual Report on Sexual Assault in the Military, (2015).

72 Tripp, T. (2016). A Body-Based Bilateral Art Protocol for Reprocessing Trauma. In J. L. King (Ed.), *Art therapy, trauma and neuroscience: Theoretical and practical perspectives.* Basingstoke: Taylor & Francis. (p. 174)

73 Kolk, B. A. (2015). *The body keeps the score: Mind, brain and body in the transformation of trauma.* London: Penguin Books. (p. 240)

74 Kolk, B. A. (2015). *The body keeps the score: Mind, brain and body in the transformation of trauma.* London: Penguin Books. (p. 240)

75 https://definitions.uslegal.com/o/order-of-protection/

76 https://www.womenslaw.org/laws/il/restraining-orders

77 https://www.rainn.org/statistics/perpetrators-sexual-violence

78 https://statesofincarceration.org/story/thinking-through-incarceration-and-sexual-violence

79 https://statesofincarceration.org/story/thinking-through-incarceration-and-sexual-violence

80 https://www.brainline.org/article/dsm-5-criteria-ptsd

81 https://www.hrc.org/resources/sexual-assault-and-the-lgbt-community

82 1. https://www.rainn.org/statistics/victims-sexual-violence David Cantor, Bonnie Fisher, Susan Chibnall, Reanna Townsend, et. al. Association of American Universities (AAU), Report on the AAU Campus Climate Survey on Sexual Assault and Sexual Misconduct (September 21, 2015). (*"Victim services agency"* is defined in this study as a *"public or privately funded organization that provides victims with support and services to aid their recovery, offer protection, guide them through the criminal justice process, and assist with obtaining restitution."* RAINN presents this data for educational purposes only, and strongly recommends using the citations to review any and all sources for more information and detail.)

83 https://www.cdc.gov/violenceprevention/pdf/cdc_nisvs_victimization_final-a.pdf

84 https://www.cdc.gov/violenceprevention/pdf/cdc_nisvs_victimization_final-a.pdf

85 https://www.hrc.org/resources/sexual-assault-and-the-lgbt-community

86 https://rapecrisis.org.za/rape-trauma-syndrome/

87 https://rapecrisis.org.za/rape-trauma-syndrome/

88 https://www.kcsarc.org/sites/default/files/Resources%20-%20Rape%20Trauma%20Syndrome.pdf

89 https://rapecrisis.org.za/rape-trauma-syndrome/

90 Johnson, N.L., & Johnson, D. M. (2017). An Empirical Exploration Into the Measurement of Rape Culture. *Journal of Interpersonal Violence*, 088626051773234. Doi: 10.1177/0886260517732347

91 Johnson, N.L., & Johnson, D. M. (2017). An Empirical Exploration Into the Measurement of Rape Culture. *Journal of Interpersonal Violence*, 088626051773234. Doi: 10.1177/0886260517732347

92 https://www.rainn.org/articles/rape-kit

93 https://www.merriam-webster.com/dictionary/resilience?utm_campaign=sd&utm_medium=serp&utm_source=jsonld

94 https://www.justice.gov/ovw/sexual-assault#sa

95 Johnson, N.L., & Johnson, D. M. (2017). An Empirical Exploration Into the Measurement of Rape Culture. *Journal of Interpersonal Violence*, 088626051773234. Doi: 10.1177/0886260517732347

96 https://apps.rainn.org/policy/

97 https://www.who.int/hiv/topics/vct/sw_toolkit/115solution.pdf

98 http://swopusa.org/

99 https://www.rainn.org/articles/key-terms-and-phrases

100 https://www.advocate.com/women/2017/12/11/what-toxic-masculinity

101 https://www.advocate.com/women/2017/12/11/what-toxic-masculinity

102 https://www.salon.com/2016/06/13/overcompensation_nation_its_time_to_admit_that_toxic_masculinity_drives_gun_violence/

103 https://www.vice.com/en_us/article/zmk3ej/all-masculinity-is-toxic

104 https://www.nij.gov/topics/crime/human-trafficking/pages/welcome.aspx

105 http://www.endslaverynow.org/learn/slavery-today/sex-trafficking

106 https://www.merriam-webster.com/dictionary/trigger

107 I.   Department of Justice, Office of Justice Programs, Bureau of Justice Statistics, National Crime Victimization Survey, 2010-2014 (2015);

II. Federal Bureau of Investigation, National Incident-Based Reporting System, 2012-2014 (2015);

III. Federal Bureau of Investigation, National Incident-Based Reporting System, 2012-2014 (2015);

IV. Department of Justice, Office of Justice Programs, Bureau of Justice Statistics, Felony Defendants in Large Urban Counties, 2009 (2013).

(This statistic combines information from several federal government reports. Because it combines data from studies with different methodologies, it is an approximation, not a scientific estimate. Please see the original sources for more detailed information. These statistics are updated annually and as new information is published.)

108 1.   Department of Justice, Office of Justice Programs, Bureau of Justice Statistics, Rape and Sexual Victimization Among College-Aged Females, 1995-2013 (2014).

109 1.   Department of Justice, Office of Justice Programs, Bureau of Justice Statistics, Crimes Against the Elderly, 2003-2013 (2014).

110 1.   Department of Defense, Fiscal Year 2014 Annual Report on Sexual Assault in the Military (2015).

111 Lipsky, L. V., & Burk, C. (2009). *Trauma stewardship: An everyday guide to caring for self while caring for others.* Oakland, CA: Berrett-Koehler.

112 https://definitions.uslegal.com/v/victim-blaming/

113 https://volopps.rainn.org/

114 https://endsexualviolencect.org/resources/get-the-facts/woc-stats/

115 1.   Department of Justice, Office of Justice Programs, Bureau of Justice Statistics, American Indians and Crime, 1992-2002 (2004).

116 https://www.merriam-webster.com/dictionary/xenophobia

117 tps://www.thedailybeast.com/the-right-wings-xenophobic-feminism?ref=scroll

118 Emerson, D. & Hopper, E. (2011). *Overcoming trauma through yoga: Reclaiming your body.* Berkeley, CA: North Atlantic Books.

More Publications on the Subject:

Dieterich-Hartwell, Rebekka. (2017). Dance/Movement Therapy in the Treatment of Post Traumatic Stress: A Reference Model. *The Arts in Psychotherapy.* 54.10.1016/j.aip.2017.02.010.

Gantt, L., & Tinnin, L. W. (2009). Support for a neurobiological view of trauma with implications for art therapy. *The Arts in Psychotherapy,* 36(3), 148-153. Doi: 10.1016/j.aip.2008.12.005

Goodman, R. D., PhD, LPC. (2015). *A Liberatory Approach to Trauma Counseling: Decolonizing Our Trauma-Informed Practices.* 55-72. 10.1007/978-1-4939-1283-4_5.

Hass-Cohen, N., & Findlay, J. C. (2015). Art therapy & the neuroscience of relationships, creativity, & resiliency: Skills and practices. New York: W.W. Norton & Company.

Herman, J. L. (2015). *Trauma and recovery: The aftermath of violence, from domestic abuse to political terror.* New York: Basic Books, a member of the Perseus Books Group.

Johnson, N.L., & Johnson, D. M. (2017). An Empirical Exploration Into the Measurement of Rape Culture. *Journal of Interpersonal Violence,* 088626051773234. Doi: 10.1177/0886260517732347

Tripp, T. (2016). A Body-Based Bilateral Art Protocol for Reprocessing Trauma. In J. L. King (Ed.), *Art therapy, trauma and neuroscience: Theoretical and practical perspectives.* Basingstoke: Taylor & Francis.

Kolk, B. A. (2015). *The body keeps the score: Mind, brain and body in the transformation of trauma.* London: Penguin Books.

Lerner, G. (1992). *Black women in white America: A documentary history.* New York: Vintage Books.

Levine, P. A. (1997). *Waking the tiger: Healing trauma: The innate capacity to transform overwhelming experiences.* Berkeley, CA: North Atlantic Books.

Emerson, D. & Hopper, E. (2011). *Overcoming trauma through yoga: Reclaiming your body.* Berkeley, CA: North Atlantic Books.

Porges, S. W. (2017). *The pocket guide to the polyvagal theory: The transformative power of feeling safe.* New York: W.W. Norton.

Siegel, D. J. (2012). *The developing mind: Second edition.* New York, NY: TheGuilford Press.

Other Resources:

justbeinc.wixsite.com/justbeinc/the-me-too-movement-c7cf

valor.us/2009/11/01/history-of-the-rape-crisis-movement/

slate.com/human-interest/2018/02/how-formerly-enslaved-black-women-fought-for-human-dignity-and-sexual-justice.html

plannedparenthood.org/learn/relationships/sexual-consent

Americanarttherapyassociation.org

Americandancetherapyassociation.org

Forge.org

Ourresilience.org

RAINN.org

Seekthenspeak.org

Startbybelieving.org

Upsettingrapeculture.org

Victimlink.org

YWCA.org

Printed in the United States
by Baker & Taylor Publisher Services